Working Horses

Therapy Horses

by Rachel Grack

Bullfrog Books

Ideas for Parents and Teachers

Bullfrog Books let children practice reading informational text at the earliest reading levels. Repetition, familiar words, and photo labels support early readers.

Before Reading

Discuss the cover photo. What does it tell them?

Look at the picture glossary together. Read and discuss the words.

Read the Book

"Walk" through the book and look at the photos. Let the child ask questions. Point out the photo labels.

Read the book to the child, or have him or her read independently.

After Reading

Prompt the child to think more. Ask: Did you know about therapy horses before reading this book? What more would you like to learn about them?

Bullfrog Books are published by Jump!
5357 Penn Avenue South
Minneapolis, MN 55419
www.jumplibrary.com

Library of Congress Cataloging-in-Publication Data

Names: Koestler-Grack, Rachel A., 1973– author.
Title: Therapy horses / by Rachel Grack.
Description: Minneapolis, MN: Jump!, Inc., [2024]
Series: Working horses | Includes index.
Audience: Ages 5–8
Identifiers: LCCN 2022052122 (print)
LCCN 2022052123 (ebook)
ISBN 9798885245029 (hardcover)
ISBN 9798885245036 (paperback)
ISBN 9798885245043 (ebook)
Subjects: LCSH: Animals as aids for people with disabilities—Juvenile literature.
Horses—Therapeutic use—Juvenile literature.
Classification: LCC RM931.H6 K64 2024 (print)
LCC RM931.H6 (ebook)
DDC 362.4/0483—dc23/eng/20221117
LC record available at https://lccn.loc.gov/2022052122
LC ebook record available at https://lccn.loc.gov/2022052123

Editor: Katie Chanez
Designer: Molly Ballanger

Photo Credits: Kuznetsov Dmitriy/Shutterstock, cover; Liudmila Chernetska/iStock, 1; Jevtic/iStock, 3; martinedoucet/iStock, 4, 5, 23tm, 23br; Kathleen Flynn/The Tampa Bay Times/AP Images, 6–7; ABK/BSIP/BSIP/SuperStock, 8–9, 14–15, 22br, 23tr, 23bl; Ben Welsh/Design Pics/SuperStock, 10–11, 23tl; AnnGaysorn/Shutterstock, 12, 13; Pipa100/Dreamstime, 16, 17; Air_Lady/Shutterstock, 18–19; AMELIE-BENOIST/BSIP/BSIP /SuperStock, 20–21; Khilinichenko Yurii/Shutterstock, 22tl; Dmitryp-k/Shutterstock, 22tr; mgstudyo/iStock, 22bl; Vac1/Shutterstock, 23bm; cynoclub/Shutterstock, 24.

Printed in the United States of America at Corporate Graphics in North Mankato, Minnesota.

Table of Contents

Helping Pals

Lady is a therapy horse.

She helps Ava.

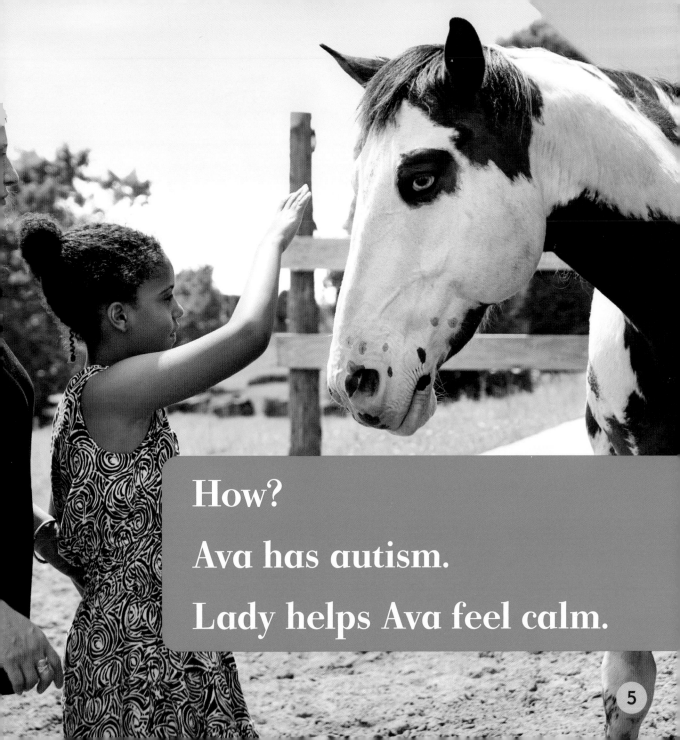

How?

Ava has autism.

Lady helps Ava feel calm.

Therapy horses are friendly.
Champ lets kids ride!

Lee is blind.

He brushes Doc.

Doc stays still.

They trust each other.

brush

Kat was anxious.

She washes Sky.

Now Kat feels calm.

It is hard for
Max to sit up.

12

He rides Bo.

He gets stronger.

13

cart

14

Dan cannot walk.

He sits in a cart.

He takes a ride!

Mia is shy.

She leads Ace.

She is proud.

Good job!

It is hard for Joe to move.

He lies on Ed's back.

Ed walks.

It moves Joe's muscles.

Horses help.
They are great pals.
Thank you!

On the Job

Take a look at some of the ways therapy horses help!

People brush, feed, or care for horses. It helps people feel calm and builds trust.

People sit or lie on horses' backs to help strengthen muscles.

People ride horses for fun. It also helps their bodies grow stronger.

People who can't ride horses can ride in carts pulled by horses.

Picture Glossary

anxious
Feeling worried
or scared.

autism
A condition that can
cause communication
and behavioral
challenges.

blind
Not able to see or
able to see very little.

cart
A small wagon with
two or four wheels
pulled by an animal.

muscles
Tissues in the body
that help us move.

therapy
Having to do with
treatment for an illness,
injury, disability, or
mental health issue.

Index

To Learn More

Finding more information is as easy as 1, 2, 3.

❶ Go to www.factsurfer.com

❷ Enter "therapyhorses" into the search box.

❸ Choose your book to see a list of websites.